M000049550

ASTROLOGY GEMS

CANCER
June 21 – July 22

Monte Farber & Amy Zerner

Sterling Publishing Co., Inc.
New York

Text © 2006 by Monte Farber
Art © 2006 by Amy Zerner

10 9 8 7 6 5 4 3

Published by Sterling Publishing Co., Inc.
387 Park Avenue South, New York, NY 10016

Distributed in Canada by Sterling Publishing
c/o Canadian Manda Group, 165 Dufferin Street
Toronto, Ontario, Canada M6K 3H6

Distributed in the United Kingdom by GMC
Distribution Services
Castle Place, 166 High Street, Lewes, East Sussex,
England BN7 1XU

Distributed in Australia by Capricorn Link (Australia)
Pty. Ltd.
P.O. Box 704, Windsor, NSW 2756, Australia

Printed in China

Sterling ISBN-13: 978-1-4027-4177-7
        ISBN-10: 1-4027-4177-4

For information about custom editions, special sales,
premium and corporate purchases, please contact
Sterling Special Sales Department at 800-805-5489 or
specialsales@sterlingpub.com.

What's Your Sign?

When someone asks you "What's your sign?" you know what that person really means is "What's your astrological sign?" Professional astrologers more often use the phrase "Sun sign," a term reflecting the concept that a person's sign is determined by which of the twelve signs of the zodiac the Sun appeared to be passing through at the moment she was born. The zodiac is the narrow band of sky circling the Earth's equator through which the Sun, the Moon, and the planets appear to move when viewed by us here on Earth.

Astrology's Gift

Astrology, which has been around for thousands of years, is the study of how planetary positions relate to earthly events and people. Its long and rich history has resulted in a wealth of philosophical and psychological wisdom, the basic concepts of which we are going to share with you in the pages of this book. As the Greek philosopher Heracleitus (c. 540–c. 480 BCE) said, "Character is destiny." Who you are—complete with all of your goals, tendencies, habits, virtues, and vices—will

determine how you act and react, thereby creating your life's destiny. Like astrology itself, our Astrology Gems series is designed to help you to better know yourself and those you care about. You will then be better able to use your free will to shape your life to your liking.

Does Astrology Work?

Many people rightly question how astrology can divide humanity into twelve Sun signs and make predictions that can be correct for everyone of the same sign. The simple answer is that it cannot do that—that's newspaper astrology, entertaining but not the real thing. Rather, astrology can help you understand your strengths and weaknesses so that you can better accept yourself as you are and use your strengths to compensate for your weaknesses. Real astrology is designed to help you to become yourself fully.

Remember, virtually all the music in the history of Western music has been composed using variations of the same twelve notes. Similarly, the twelve Sun signs of astrology are basic themes rich with meaning that each of us expresses differently to create and respond to the unique opportunities and challenges of our life.

CANCER

June 21–July 22

Planet
Moon

Element
Water

Quality
Cardinal

Day
Monday

Season
summer

Colors
silver, mauve, smoke gray

Plants
moonflower, water lily, chamomile

Perfume
sandalwood

Gemstones
moonstone, pearl, opal, hematite

Metal
silver

Personal qualities
Caring, tenacious, sensitive, intuitive,
and practical

We call the following words "keywords" because they can help you unlock the core meaning of the astrological sign of Cancer. Each keyword represents issues and ideas that are of supreme importance and prominence in the lives of people born with Cancer as their Sun sign. You will usually find that a Cancer embodies at least one of these keywords in the way she makes a living:

nurturing   fertile   clairvoyant

protective • heredity   farming

emotions • moods

consumerism • feelings

intuitions • wax and wane

reflect • respond • adapt

habits • cycles • motherhood

unconditional love • our past

cooking • home making

passivity • memories of childhood

caregiving • secrets

conservation   leadership

love of comfort   patriotism

antiques   surrogacy

women's issues

Cancer's Symbolic Meaning

The symbol for Cancer is the Crab. Cancerians have a tendency to feel insecure at times, and when they experience this emotion they want to withdraw into their own version of a crab's protective shell. A crab carries its home on its back wherever it goes, and in much the same way, a Cancerian strives to make a metaphorical home out of even the most temporary surroundings.

The desire to nurture and protect loved ones is very strong in every Cancer and is borne out by the sign's designation as the Great Mother. The issue of people providing or failing to provide material support will be a central focus of every person born during the time of the sign of Cancer.

Cancer is one of the four Cardinal signs of the zodiac (the other three are Aries, Libra, and Capricorn). Cardinal signs are the first signs in each season. Thus, those born under these signs are initiators and act according to their aims and goals.

Although they can be gentle and shy, they are also tenacious, and will fight hard to get what they want. But because they are quiet and well mannered, they are able to accomplish their aims without seeming to be pushy or demanding.

Additionally, Cancer is one of the three Water signs (the other two being Scorpio and Pisces). People whose signs fall into this group are highly imaginative and emotional. Cancer is the Water sign concerned with protection, caring, and comfort. Cancerians are legendary for their ability to nurture people and projects, for they sense the needs of others on an emotional level. However, they need to remember that meeting their own emotional needs is just as important. Often, they must be able to nurture themselves, for they are so good at nurturing others that those other people forget that Cancerians, too, need similar attention.

Cancerians would do well to remember that while they may not be as strong as those around them think they are, they are certainly strong enough to do what has to be done to make their dreams come true. They must resist withdrawing into their shell if they start to feel insecure. Their usual courage, patience, and gentle energy are more than they need to make their life what they will.

Recognizing a Cancer

People who exhibit the physical characteristics distinctive of the sign of Cancer have expressive eyes, a round "moon-shaped" face, and soft skin. Every mood, emotion, and fleeting response shows in the changing features of the sensitive Cancerian face. Those born under this sign are usually top heavy, and their arms and legs tend to be long in relation to the rest of their body. They can often be on the plump side, especially later in life.

Cancer's Typical Behavior and Personality Traits

❋ desirous of material comforts

❋ extremely clairvoyant

❋ wears clothes that feel protective

❋ is a bit shy (not a show-off)

❋ private about personal life

❋ wonderful with children

❋ introspective and emotional

❋ possesses a shrewd business sense

- enjoys good food and wine
- protective of friends and family
- patient and cautious with decisions
- gets her feelings hurt easily
- dreamy, subtle, and intuitive

What Makes a Cancer Tick?

More than those born under any other sign, Cancerians are driven by feelings and intuition. Even though they are intelligent, practical people, they use their feelings as a sort of radar, and a great many of their decisions are based on this radar. While highly sensitive in the way they behave toward others, Cancerians are usually most sensitive when it comes to their own feelings. They are easily hurt by actions or attitudes that other signs are likely to dismiss. Hurt a Cancer and there is a chance that he will sulk.

The Cancer Personality Expressed Positively

Cancerians who possess high self-esteem and confidence may not seem much different from those who do not. But they, themselves, will certainly know the difference. The ability to sympathize with a friend's problems and still feel comfortable with their own success is a sign that Cancerians are able to balance their emotions, expressing their true nature in a positive way.

On a Positive Note

Cancers displaying the positive characteristics associated with their sign also tend to be:

* savvy

* kind

* warm

* compassionate

* nurturing

* thoughtful

* caring and sensitive

* introspective

* intuitive

The Cancer Personality Expressed Negatively

Moodiness, sulkiness, and an unwillingness to be open with others about their problems are just a few ways in which Cancerians express their personality in a negative way. These characteristics may surface when they are feeling bad about themselves or unequal to what is expected of them. Cancerians who don't feel good about themselves may become secretive or even deceptive.

Negative Traits

Cancers displaying the negative characteristics associated with their sign also tend to be:

* possessive

* controlling

* crabby

* too easily hurt

* sensitive to criticism

* manipulative

* overpowering

* selfish

* defensive

Ask a Cancer If...

Ask a Cancer if she'll listen if you want to share intimate feelings or events of a confidential nature but don't wish to be judged. Cancers pride themselves on being both empathetic and trustworthy and will listen to your problems or concerns with an open mind and an open heart. They also have the gift of giving counsel without lecturing, and will offer that service if you ask. If not, they will simply listen or provide a shoulder to cry on.

Cancers As Friends

There is no one who is more giving than a Cancer who feels secure emotionally. However, when those born under the sign of the Crab feel insecure, they are totally unable to give, and their resulting behavior can confuse friends who have come to depend on them at critical times.

On the Cancer's part, his sensitivity can lead to emotional moments with friends and his feelings being hurt. Cancerians are reluctant to tell anyone about their own needs for fear that the people they care about will let them down.

Cancerians have long memories. While they would be able to forgive a friend who was unable to be there for them, they would never forget what happened. In general, Cancerians like people who will support their emotional needs when necessary—and when they find this, they'll reciprocate.

Looking for Love

Cancerians may be attracted to an individual who reminds them of someone they used to care about. They tend to be highly romantic and dramatic in their love life, and will respond to honest warmth and affection. They can easily become tenaciously attached to someone who has no intention of making a commitment and therefore cannot return their feelings. They believe in falling in love at first sight, and if they meet someone without experiencing this sensation, it may be hard for them to believe that the person is really meant for them.

Cancerians think that magic is a big part of romance, so if this element is missing, there may be little chance of a relationship getting off the ground. Also, Cancerians sometimes hold back because they fear rejection and, therefore, may lose out on their quest for love.

Shyness can be Cancer's obstacle to finding love. Even when Cancerians think someone they like may feel the same way, it can be difficult for them to summon the courage to speak up. They are not the sort to casually meet someone and trust that the connection has the potential to go further. Nor are they the type for going out every night. They are real homebodies, and will rarely make the first move. Love may just have to come knock on their door or they may meet a romantic interest through family or close friends. Once Cancerians have found a love interest, they will put that person first. They enjoy looking after the one they love and will "mother" them in some way. It's difficult for Cancerians to understand that a lover could consider this sort of treatment smothering. To them, it is simply love.

Finding That Special Someone

In the search for a love interest, comfort is a key factor. Cancerians are rarely happy barhopping or participating in the online dating scene. Rather, they are more likely to find themselves drawn to someone they meet at work, church, or a party given by a friend. Sometimes they find that the person of their dreams has been under their nose all the time—a friend or an associate.

First Dates

An ideal first date for Cancer is likely to involve a home-cooked meal or other domestic trappings. While this type of date may seem too emotionally intimate for some, Cancerians know how to make the experience nonthreatening. Other favorable venues include a stroll on the beach, a trip to an amusement park, or an evening spent in an intimate jazz or comedy club. Cancerians are more interested in the company than the accoutrements—another expression of their down-to-earth attitude and spirit.

Cancer in Love

When Cancerians are with a partner, they should feel at home and have no need to be anywhere else.

They should spend time making their home into the kind of nest where a great relationship can be nurtured and grow strong. When they do set out on the road with a lover, they should visit a place from their past, or go to a hotel that feels like a home away from home. Cancerians are sentimental and enjoy showering their lover with attention. They show affection freely, but may restrict kissing and cuddling to private time.

Undying Love

At the first sign of ridicule or criticism, Cancerians will retreat, deeply hurt. Any problems Cancerians have in their love life are probably the result of childhood experiences. Cancer and his partner might come from completely different upbringings or one or both may have had serious traumas as children. If a Cancer is unable to forgive—especially his mother—he should consider professional counseling. If a Cancer is unable to forgive, his romantic relationships will be perpetually sabotaged by unresolved emotional problems.

Expectations in Love

Issues of mothering and nurturing are important in any Cancer's life. They may be looking for someone to take care of them or may be repelled by anyone who needs to be taken care of in some way. It may be hard to find a partner who shares a Cancer's views on children and child rearing. They are traditionalists, and if their own upbringing was happy, they will use it as their model.

Cancerians need to know that they are with someone who loves them and upon whom they can depend. This is paramount; they need to be supported, nurtured, and loved unconditionally. Although they are strong and capable people, they sometimes feel extremely vulnerable, and need to nurture their partner in order to make themselves feel safe and strong. They should be on the lookout for someone who embodies the same loving, gentle qualities. If that kind of relationship is not attractive to a Cancer, she may equate intensity, uncertainty, and even danger with passion and love, due to a difficult, dysfunctional upbringing.

What Cancerians Look For

Cancerians need a partner who appreciates their hard work, their nurturing personality, and their involvement with family. Totally devoted once they commit to a love affair, they expect the same kind of loyalty in return. Cancerians need to be needed. Cancerians like to have others—whether they be children, best friends, or family members—around them. A couple may even work closely together, and when they do, the others involved in the business can become like family to them.

If Cancerians Only Knew...

If Cancerians only knew how strong and dependable they appear to others, they wouldn't worry about letting someone close to them, especially a love interest, get a peek at their vulnerabilities. For the most part, other people perceive only the powerful will and self-discipline of Cancer. Yet Cancerians often feel weak simply because they are so sensitive. This is odd, since it is precisely that sensitivity that gives them the ability to reach out to other people in ways that are so special and so spiritually pure.

Marriage

The past is very important to Cancerians. Their family history is especially so, either as a source of pride or because of a painful experience that continues to affect them as if it just happened. Either way, Cancerians want to relate what is going on in the present to something they have known in the past. By doing this, or by simply sticking with the familiar, they are able to feel secure.

The person who contemplates marrying a typical Cancer must realize that that person will want to be the dominant partner and will expect total devotion. That said, the person who pairs up with a Cancer can expect consideration, prosperity, and a strong sense of being part of a family. The contented Cancerian will never let a partner down, stressing a sense of belonging as well as love.

Cancer's Opposite Sign

Capricorn, the Goat, is the opposite sign of Cancer. It is a hard and flinty sign possessing many of the strengths that Cancer isn't likely to have. But it is through those very differences that Capricorn can teach Cancer to be strong and emotionally self-sufficient. Capricorn, in turn, can learn from Cancer the ways to be sensitive and caring, as well as how to accept the emotional nurturing that Capricorn is likely to require.

Pairing Up

In general, if people display the characteristics typical of their sign, intimate relationships between a Cancer and another individual can be described as follows:

Cancer with Cancer
Harmonious, if there isn't too much emotional baggage

Cancer with Leo
Harmonious, so long as Leo gets plenty of attention

Cancer with Virgo
Harmonious, with both partners supporting each other's dreams

Cancer with Libra
Difficult, but enhanced by shared
life-view and goals

Cancer with Scorpio
Harmonious—deeply sensual and
eternally romantic

Cancer with Sagittarius
Turbulent but joyous, with lots of
fights and makeup sessions

Cancer with Capricorn
Difficult, although there is much for
each to learn from the other

Cancer with Aquarius
Turbulent, especially if there are
political and philosophical differences

Cancer with Pisces
Harmonious, with shared sensitivity
and romantic idealism

Cancer with Aries
Difficult but exciting, though Aries
needs to be tender

Cancer with Taurus
Harmonious in the extreme—a match
made in paradise

Cancer with Gemini
Harmonious, if Gemini gives Cancer
plenty of emotional space

If Things Don't Work Out

In modern psychology emphasis has been placed on getting in touch with childhood experiences. Only recently has equal emphasis been placed on taking responsibility for who you are now. Cancer needs to learn from the past but live in the present.

Cancerians' relationships reflect their emotional intelligence. How Cancer and his partner express their emotions will determine how well things are going. If a relationship breaks up, Cancer will shoulder most of the blame.

Cancer at Work

Cancerians need to feel that they are doing more than just a job; they want to feel more like they have found a home. They like work that reminds them of the work done by their family in the past. A sense of continuity is very important to them. Family and those who care deeply about them can help their job and career in some way. Cancerians may also work out of their home.

Cancers must feel emotionally comfortable and secure in the workplace. This means having lots of family photos and some special mementos displayed, lots of snacks and water handy, and bins and boxes to organize clutter.

A woman, matters related to women and children, mothering, mother figures, and possibly the Cancer's own mother can affect her career in an important way. If relations with women and a Cancer's mother are good, the career will benefit. If not, there can be emotional troubles that appear at work, so a Cancer should be aware of and try to heal the issues in that relationship.

Cancerians must also be on good terms with coworkers to feel secure and get their career moving properly. People who are considered "family" at work and how Cancerians have been getting along with them are very important to their professional life. If those relationships have been difficult, a Cancer must take action to make things better. Until things have been straightened out, the Cancer's career will feel blocked.

Typical Occupations

Occupations that Cancerians are well suited for address the basic needs of families, from spirituality to housework. They make excellent chefs and caterers and also housekeepers. Many find their calling in real estate.

All jobs with children or that involve nurturing people would be beneficial to them. Thus, they may succeed in anything from social work to nursing. And working with animals and gardens will be favored by them. Cancerians' nurturing capabilities also apply to fostering new business projects that are struggling to survive. Excellent organizers with a sense of value and economics, they are often successful in industry.

Those born under the sign of the Crab have an intuitive sense that makes them good counselors and journalists. The sign's love of the past makes some Cancerians great history buffs, and others astute collectors of antiques and curios. True to their native element, some of the people born under this Water sign become involved in marine activities.

Details, Details

Cancers thrive on details as long as these small, daily elements of work, and life for that matter, support a bigger, more comprehensive plan of action. They are not overly logical, and yet they have an instinct for statistics, dates, and budgetary items. Thanks to their natural talent for organization, Cancers rarely get bogged down in details. They are much more likely to see them as the underpinnings of an important and profitable enterprise.

In the workplace, Cancers do not feel as though they are "above" handling the small details that make up a big project. Dogged and determined, they will slog away at the difficult elements of a project, never worrying about whether or not they will end up getting credit for the final results. This has nothing to do with a lack of ego on their part. They know that they have the ability to work as a team member better than many of their coworkers,

Behavior and Abilities at Work

In the workplace, a typical Cancer:

- is loyal and efficient
- excels as either a leader or a team member
- gets along well with others in the workplace
- may be resistant to new ideas
- has the company's interests at heart

Cancer As Employer

A typical Cancer boss:

- drives a hard bargain but is fair
- treats employees like family
- expects employees to dress nicely
- takes work seriously
- does not like silliness
- focuses on making money
- possesses an excellent memory
- likes to reward loyalty

Cancer As Employee

A typical Cancer employee:

- likes to be given responsibility
- has goals of increasing income
- expects to be rewarded for hard work
- is good at sales and marketing
- will have a calm and considerate personality
- uses intuition more than logic
- enjoys being part of a "family"

Cancer As Coworker

Making others feel like they are part of the group is crucial for Cancerians. However, Cancerians may sometimes pull back from having close ties in the workplace. They may fear sharing the intimate details of their own personal life with others. Since they feel vulnerable to criticism or judgment, Cancerians are less likely than other signs to gossip.

Money

Whether a Cancer lives in a cave or a castle, making it beautiful, comfortable, and safe would be money well spent. Collecting original art would feed a Cancer's soul, something that is necessary to achieve true wealth and success.

Cancer's financial resources are likely to come from or be connected to organizations related to the home, products for the home, the past, or family values. If a Cancer wants to enter any lotteries, he would do better to enter with close friends and family. Numbers important to family members would be the most likely to be lucky. A Cancer should try to profit from the advice of family and people from the past and from long-term investments. Real estate, especially a property a Cancer or his family intends to live on, is a good bet. Any improvements that a Cancer makes to where he lives will be good investments, too.

At Home

In order to nurture the ones they love, Cancerians must first feel secure. They want their home to be comfortable, a true sanctuary where they can relax and enjoy family life and activities. Because Cancer is the Cardinal Water sign, it follows that emotion in action is the key to understanding how Cancerians relax.

Behavior and Abilities at Home

Cancer typically:

* enjoys feeling safe and relaxed

* is handy with home improvements

* enjoys entertaining guests

* has lots of cookbooks

* has plants or a garden

* may have collections of family heirlooms

* doesn't like to throw things away

Leisure
Interests

Cancerians may join health clubs, but they prefer yoga, swimming, and meditation to weight lifting and aerobics. They enjoy relaxing on the beach with a good book. And they love to just hang out with friends and family, enjoying a good meal, surrounded by the warmth of a contented atmosphere.

The typical Cancer enjoys the following pastimes:

- gardening or tending plants
- playing with his pets
- collecting antiques
- engaging in team sports or playing games
- keeping a journal
- boating, sailing, or swimming

Cancerian Likes

- anyone who has a kind heart
- mementos from family and friends
- comfort food
- shopping sprees
- history and psychology books
- sentimental gifts
- birthday cards
- old friends
- a beautiful home
- cuddly pajamas or soft blankets

Cancerian Dislikes

- harsh words
- fast food
- people who forget important dates
- not being acknowledged for her contribution
- talking to strangers
- a messy home
- having to respond quickly, without time to think
- moving
- not having money
- being nagged at or lectured

The Secret Side of Cancer

Cancerians are often affected by the time of day they decide to do something. Plans made at night become harder to make real in the daytime and vice versa. If they find themselves forgetting to put the plans of last night into practice the next day, they must be as patient and forgiving of themselves as they would be with the mistakes made by a child.

The Moon ☽

The Moon, which is considered a planet in astrology, is associated with the sign of Cancer. The way in which the Moon seems to change size and shape, along with the Moon's effect on the constantly shifting ocean tides, resembles Cancer's ever-changing moods; however, the Moon's changes are a lot more predictable.

Astrologers of old associated the Moon with our emotions, our emotional intelligence, our intuition, and the expression of all of these things. Because it changes shape from full to new on a schedule so close to that of a woman's menstrual cycle, the Moon is associated with women, fertility, planting, childbirth, mothering, and nurturing in general. It also rules the relationship between mother and child. Watching over us all the time, though not always seen, the Moon represents our unconscious attitudes, patterns, and past conditioning. This celestial body rules the breast and stomach.

Bringing Up a Young Cancer

Cancerian children love to use their imaginations and are easy to get along with, provided they are given lots of warmth, approval, and attention. Usually gentle, complacent souls, they most of all are sure of what they want and need.

Cancerian youths needs to feel free to express their emotions through art, music, writing, or any other form of creativity. They need plenty of outlets for their vivid imaginations. Thus, young Cancerians should be taught the basic techniques of any art form and given the proper materials and space within which to be creative.

The parents of a Cancerian child must find a way not to be too possessive or overprotective. They may worry too much about their little Cancerian child, as children born under this sign are deeply sensitive to emotional hurts and rejections and are prone to withdrawing into their little shells. If the child feels unloved or neglected, she could grow up to be a reclusive, withdrawn adult who is overly self-protective and reluctant to trust or get too close to other people.

Like those born during the other Water signs, Pisces and Scorpio, Cancer children can be very intuitive; many may display what appears to be psychic abilities. Their caregivers need to value this while guiding them to develop their logical faculties too.

Cancer As a Parent

The typical Cancer parent:

* likes to make birthday parties

* supports creativity

* is overprotective

* is very reassuring when fears arise

* enjoys playing with the kids

* will do anything to help

* displays affection

The Cancer Child

The typical Cancer child:

- likes to be hugged
- may cry a lot
- changes moods from day to day
- likes to save money
- can manipulate to get what he wants
- loves mealtime
- is fascinated by picture books
- gets her feelings hurt easily
- withdraws if unhappy

- can play alone for hours
- conjures up imaginary playmates
- likes traditional fairy tales and myths

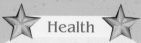

Health

Cancerians are emotional types who may suffer from stomach problems when under stress. They tend to bottle things up and are prone to ulcers. As they do not like to burden other people with their problems, they tend to suffer in silence. Typical Cancerians need material security, plenty of affection, and a sense that they are needed. As long as these needs are met, they can handle a lot.

Wholesome food and regular meals are important to Cancer. Overindulgence in sweets can result in extra weight gained in later years. Since theirs is a water sign, Cancerians should try taking long, warm baths to relax.

★ FAMOUS CANCERS ★

Louis Armstrong

Bill Blass

Mel Brooks

Bill Cosby

Tom Cruise

Diana, Princess of Wales

Harrison Ford

Bob Fosse

John Glenn

Tom Hanks

Ernest Hemingway

Frida Kahlo

Lindsay Lohan

Nelson Mandela

George Orwell

Gilda Radner

Ginger Rogers

Carlos Santana

Carly Simon

Sylvester Stallone

Ringo Starr

Meryl Streep

Robin Williams

THE ENCHANTED WORLD of AMY ZERNER & MONTE FARBER

About the Authors

Internationally known self-help author Monte Farber's inspiring guidance and empathic insights impact everyone he encounters. Amy Zerner's exquisite one-of-a-kind spiritual couture creations and collaged fabric paintings exude her profound intuition and deep connection with archetypal stories and healing energies. Together, they have built The Enchanted World of Amy Zerner and Monte Farber: books, card decks, and

oracles that have helped millions discover their own spiritual paths.

Their best-selling titles include The Chakra Meditation Kit, The Enchanted Tarot, The Instant Tarot Reader, The Psychic Circle, Karma Cards, The Truth Fairy, The Healing Deck, True Love Tarot, Animal Powers Meditation Kit, The Breathe Easy Deck, The Pathfinder Psychic Talking Board, and Gifts of the Goddess Affirmation Cards.

For further information, please visit: **www.TheEnchantedWorld.com**